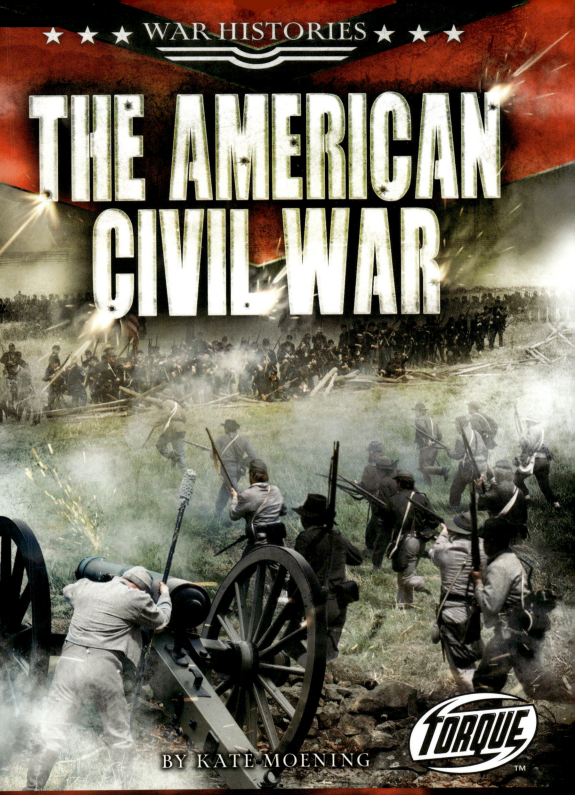

Torque brims with excitement perfect for thrill-seekers of all kinds. Discover daring survival skills, explore uncharted worlds, and marvel at mighty engines and extreme sports. In *Torque* books, anything can happen. Are you ready?

This edition first published in 2024 by Bellwether Media, Inc.

No part of this publication may be reproduced in whole or in part without written permission of the publisher. For information regarding permission, write to Bellwether Media, Inc., Attention: Permissions Department, 6012 Blue Circle Drive, Minnetonka, MN 55343.

Library of Congress Cataloging-in-Publication Data

Names: Moening, Kate, author.
Title: The American Civil War / by Kate Moening.
Other titles: War histories (Bellwether Media)
Description: Minneapolis, MN : Bellwether Media, Inc., 2024 | Series: Torque: War histories | Includes bibliographical references and index. | Audience: Ages 7-12 | Audience: Grades 4-6 | Summary: "Engaging images accompany information about the American Civil War. The combination of high-interest subject matter and light text is intended for students in grades 3 through 7" – Provided by publisher.
Identifiers: LCCN 2023007838 (print) | LCCN 2023007839 (ebook) | ISBN 9798886874501 (library binding) | ISBN 9798886875423 (paperback) | ISBN 9798886876383 (ebook)
Subjects: LCSH: United States–History–Civil War, 1861-1865–Juvenile literature. | LCGFT: Illustrated works.
Classification: LCC E468 .M575 2024 (print) | LCC E468 (ebook) | DDC 973.7–dc23/eng/20230224
LC record available at https://lccn.loc.gov/2023007838
LC ebook record available at https://lccn.loc.gov/2023007839

Text copyright © 2024 by Bellwether Media, Inc. TORQUE and associated logos are trademarks and/or registered trademarks of Bellwether Media, Inc.

Editor: Elizabeth Neuenfeldt   Designer: Josh Brink

Printed in the United States of America, North Mankato, MN.

TABLE OF CONTENTS

WHAT WAS THE AMERICAN CIVIL WAR?	4
A DIVIDED COUNTRY	6
ON THE BATTLEFIELD	8
A DIFFERENT KIND OF WAR	14
REBUILDING THE COUNTRY	18
GLOSSARY	22
TO LEARN MORE	23
INDEX	24

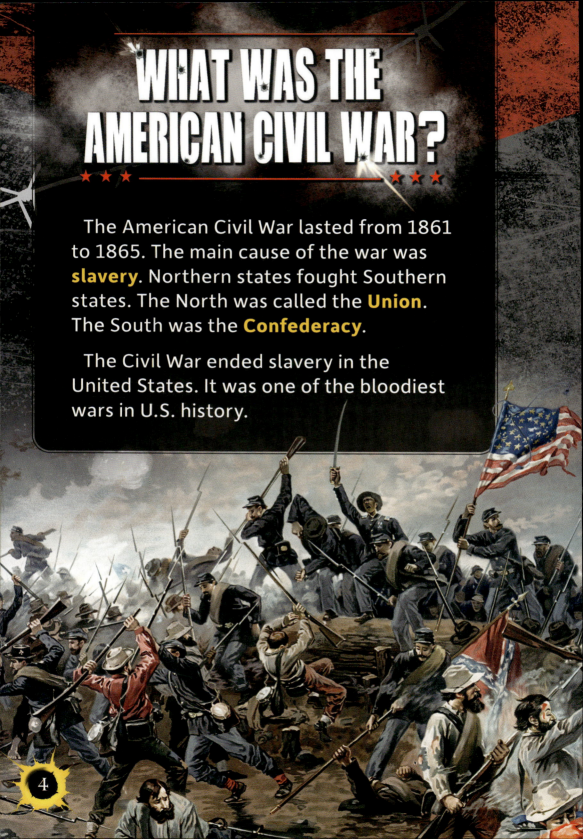

WHAT WAS THE AMERICAN CIVIL WAR?

The American Civil War lasted from 1861 to 1865. The main cause of the war was **slavery**. Northern states fought Southern states. The North was called the **Union**. The South was the **Confederacy**.

The Civil War ended slavery in the United States. It was one of the bloodiest wars in U.S. history.

AMERICAN CIVIL WAR IN 1864

Union states = 🔹
Confederate states = 🔶
border states = 🔹🔹

STATES OF THE CIVIL WAR

Twenty states fought for the North.
Eleven states fought for the South.
There were also five border states.
Slavery was legal in border states.
But these states did not secede.

A DIVIDED COUNTRY

During the 1800s, Northern states **abolished** slavery. Many Northerners wanted to end slavery across the country. But Southerners thought states should decide for themselves. The Southern **economy** relied on slavery. Tensions began to rise.

In 1860, Abraham Lincoln was **elected** president. Southerners worried Lincoln would ban slavery. Southern states began to **secede**.

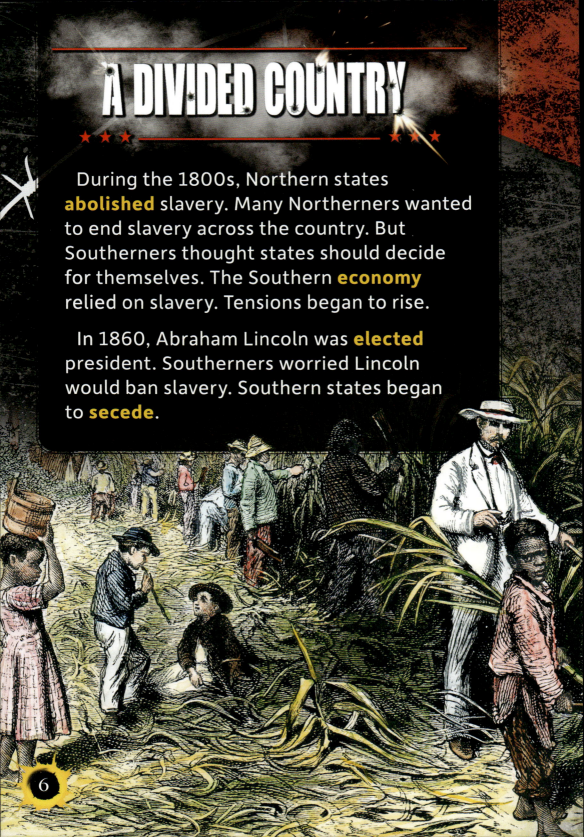

KEEPING THE COUNTRY TOGETHER

Abraham Lincoln did not want Southern states to secede. He worried it would show the world that a government by the people did not work.

ABRAHAM LINCOLN

ON THE BATTLEFIELD

In April 1861, the South attacked Fort Sumter in South Carolina. The North soon **surrendered** the fort. The war had begun.

In September 1862, the Battle of Antietam was fought in Maryland. Afterward, Lincoln announced the **Emancipation Proclamation**. It promised to end slavery. Black men could join the Northern military. It made other countries decide not to help the South.

BATTLE OF ANTIETAM

THE BATTLE OF ANTIETAM

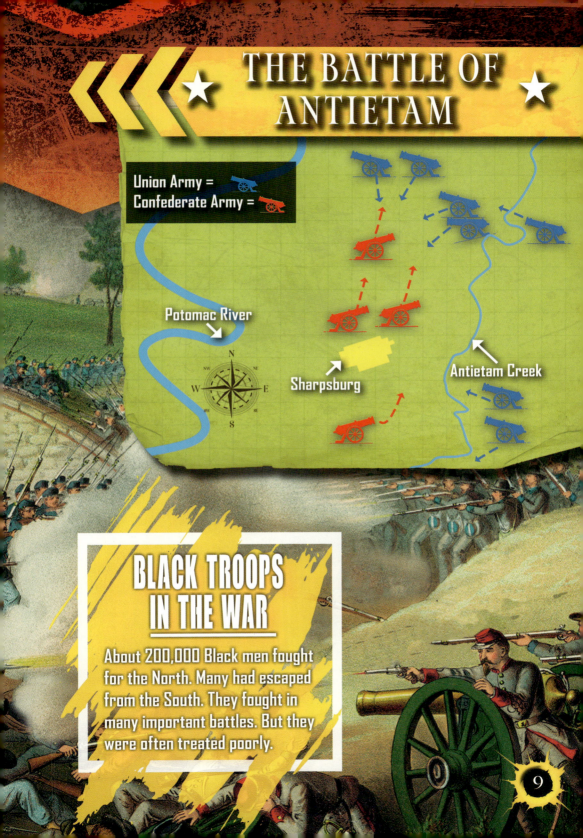

Union Army =
Confederate Army =

Potomac River
Sharpsburg
Antietam Creek

BLACK TROOPS IN THE WAR

About 200,000 Black men fought for the North. Many had escaped from the South. They fought in many important battles. But they were often treated poorly.

Soldiers often fought face-to-face. A group of soldiers marched toward the enemy in two lines. Once they were close enough, they fired their rifles. Soldiers also used cannons to fire from farther away.

Both sides had big armies. But the North's army was larger. At the peak of the war, the North had twice as many soldiers as the South.

CANNONS IN THE AMERICAN CIVIL WAR

3-inch Ordnance Rifle

1,800 YARDS | 1,600 YARDS | 1,400 YARDS | 1,200 YARDS | 1,000 YARDS | 800 YARDS | 600 YARDS | 400 YARDS | 200 YARDS

Range
range: 1,830 yards (1,673 meters)

Ammunition Used
rifled ammunition

1857 Model Napoleon

1,800 YARDS | 1,600 YARDS | 1,400 YARDS | 1,200 YARDS | 1,000 YARDS | 800 YARDS | 600 YARDS | 400 YARDS | 200 YARDS

Range
Up to 1,620 yards (1,481 meters)

Ammunition Used
smoothbore ammunition

NAVY BATTLES

Most fighting happened on land. But some battles were fought at sea and on rivers! Both sides used submarines and iron warships.

The North lost many early battles. But in May 1863, General Ulysses S. Grant began a **siege** on Vicksburg, Mississippi. Southern troops ran out of supplies. They surrendered on July 4.

UNION ARMY LEADER

NAME
Ulysses S. Grant

NATIONALITY
American (Union)

RANK
General-in-Chief

IMPORTANT ACTIONS
- 1862: Won the first major Northern victory at Fort Donelson in Tennessee

- 1863: Successfully planned and carried out the siege on Vicksburg

- 1865: Stopped Robert E. Lee's forces and ended the war

CONFEDERATE ARMY LEADER

NAME
Robert E. Lee

NATIONALITY
American (Confederacy)

RANK
General

IMPORTANT ACTIONS
- 1862: Took command of the Army of Northern Virginia

- 1862: Stopped the North from capturing the Confederate capital, Richmond, Virginia

- 1863: Led the Confederate Army to win the Battle of Chancellorsville

Meanwhile, Southern general Robert E. Lee marched to Gettysburg, Pennsylvania. It was the deadliest battle in the war. Lee lost. Southerners lost hope of winning the war.

A DIFFERENT KIND OF WAR

The Civil War was the first conflict that was photographed on a large scale. At home, people saw what war was really like. Newspapers also kept people informed.

Most battles happened in the South. The fighting made it hard to get food. Many Southern cities had **riots** over food.

THE WAR AT HOME

During the war, many women ran farms and businesses. Others became nurses in hospitals and on the battlefield.

Children also took on new jobs. They cared for younger siblings. They made clothes and blankets. In the South, some children stole food for their families.

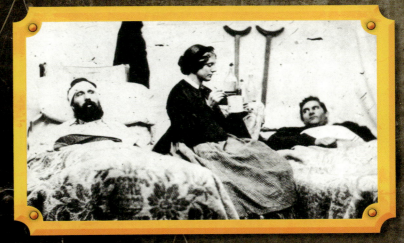

Northern general William Sherman wanted to end the war. In September 1864, he captured Atlanta, Georgia.

WILLIAM SHERMAN

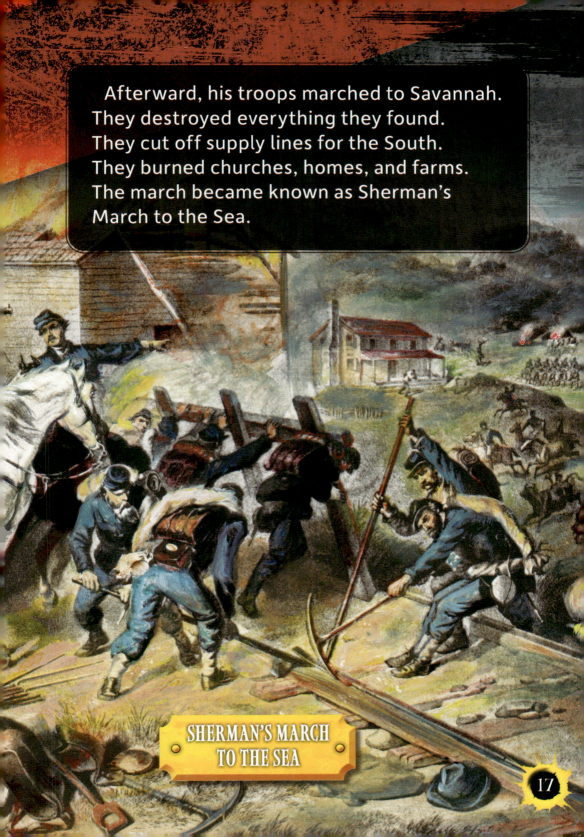

Afterward, his troops marched to Savannah. They destroyed everything they found. They cut off supply lines for the South. They burned churches, homes, and farms. The march became known as Sherman's March to the Sea.

SHERMAN'S MARCH TO THE SEA

REBUILDING THE COUNTRY

By 1865, the Confederate Army was weak. That April, the North forced General Lee out of Richmond, Virginia. Lee tried to escape to North Carolina. But General Grant stopped him.

Lee realized the South could not win. He wanted to prevent more deaths. He and Grant met in the town of Appomattox Court House. Lee surrendered. The North won the war.

AMERICAN CIVIL WAR TIMELINE

November to December 1860
Lincoln is elected and states begin to secede

April 12 to 14, 1861
Southern forces attack Fort Sumter, South Carolina

January 1, 1863
Lincoln announces the Emancipation Proclamation

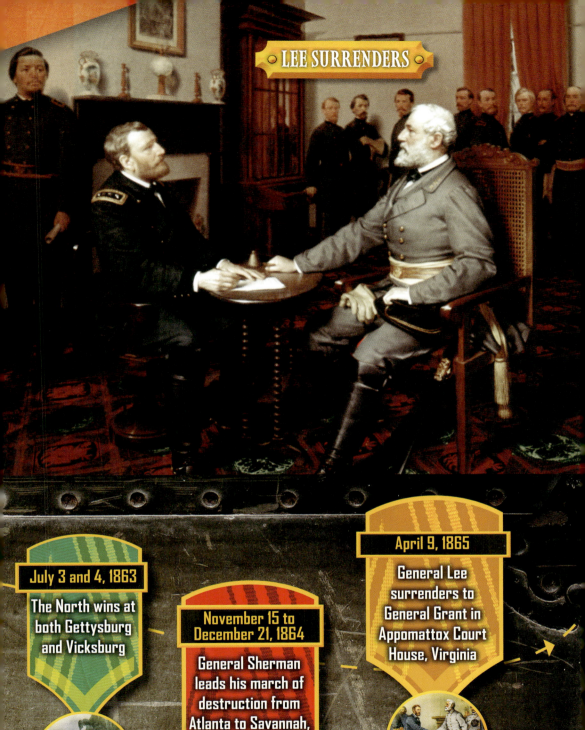

LEE SURRENDERS

July 3 and 4, 1863
The North wins at both Gettysburg and Vicksburg

November 15 to December 21, 1864
General Sherman leads his march of destruction from Atlanta to Savannah, Georgia

April 9, 1865
General Lee surrenders to General Grant in Appomattox Court House, Virginia

19

Reconstruction began after the war. The U.S. abolished slavery. More people gained citizenship. Black men could vote. But Black citizens still had fewer rights in many states.

Much of the South was in ruins. Tensions remained for a long time. But the U.S. was one nation. The war established that all people should be free.

BY THE NUMBERS

10,000 Union soldiers = 👤   10,000 Confederate soldiers = 👤

ESTIMATED CASUALTIES

- Union: 642,427
- Confederacy: 483,026

NUMBER OF STATES INVOLVED

- Union: 20
- Confederacy: 11
- border states: 5

OVERALL COST FOR THE U.S.

- Union: $3.2 billion ($80 billion in 2023 dollars)
- Confederacy: $1 billion ($21.6 billion in 2023 dollars)

ESTIMATED U.S. MILITARY PERSONNEL DEPLOYED

- Union: 2,672,341
- Confederacy: up to 1,227,890

BLACK TROOPS

- Union: around 200,000

GLOSSARY

abolished—ended or stopped

Confederacy—the group of 11 states that separated from the U.S. during the American Civil War

economy—the way a state or country makes, sells, and uses goods and services

elected—chosen by voting

Emancipation Proclamation—a document that would free the enslaved people in areas that were not under Union control as of January 1, 1863

Reconstruction—the period after the American Civil War during which Confederate states rejoined the Union and the U.S. began to rebuild; Reconstruction lasted from 1865 to 1877.

riots—situations in which large groups of people act in violent, uncontrolled ways in public

secede—to separate from a nation and form a new country

siege—a serious and lasting attack; during a siege, the military will often surround a place to force it to surrender.

slavery—the practice of forcing people to work for no pay and considering them property

surrendered—gave up power or control of something

Union—the group of northern states that supported the federal government during the American Civil War

TO LEARN MORE

AT THE LIBRARY

Kerry, Isaac. *The Attack on Fort Sumter: A Day that Changed America*. North Mankato, Minn.: Capstone Press, 2023.

Silva, Sadie. *The Civil War*. Buffalo, N.Y.: Enslow Publishing, 2023.

Smith, Elliott. *Hidden Heroes in the Civil War*. Minneapolis, Minn.: Lerner Publications, 2023.

ON THE WEB

Factsurfer.com gives you a safe, fun way to find more information.

1. Go to www.factsurfer.com

2. Enter "American Civil War" into the search box and click 🔍.

3. Select your book cover to see a list of related content.

INDEX

Appomattox Court House, 18

Atlanta, Georgia, 16

Battle of Antietam, 8, 9

Black men, 8, 9, 20

border states, 5

by the numbers, 21

cannons, 10, 11

Confederacy (South), 4, 5, 6, 7, 8, 9, 10, 12, 13, 14, 15, 17, 18, 20

Emancipation Proclamation, 8

Fort Sumter, 8

Gettysburg, Pennsylvania, 13

Grant, Ulysses S., 12, 18

leaders, 12, 13

Lee, Robert E., 13, 18, 19

Lincoln, Abraham, 6, 7, 8

map, 5, 9

navy battles, 11

newspapers, 14

photography, 14

reconstruction, 20

Richmond, Virginia, 18

riots, 14

Savannah, Georgia, 17

secede, 5, 6, 7

Sherman, William, 16, 17

Sherman's March to the Sea, 17

slavery, 4, 5, 6, 8, 20

soldiers, 10

surrender, 8, 12, 18

timeline, 18–19

troops, 12, 17

Union (North), 4, 5, 6, 8, 9, 10, 12, 16, 18

Vicksburg, Mississippi, 12

war at home, 15

weapons, 10, 11

The images in this book are reproduced through the courtesy of: William Silver, cover (cannon); Deatonphotos, cover (cannon operator); DenGuy, cover (Confederate Infantry); alancrosthwaite, cover (background Union Army); Photo Researchers/ Alamy, pp. 2-3, 4-5, 22-23, 24; North Wind Picture Archives/ Alamy, pp. 6-7, 20-21; Everett Collection, p. 7; Chronicle/ Alamy, pp. 8-9; Pictorial Press/ Alamy, pp. 10-11; Maurice Savage/ Alamy, p. 11 (3-Inch Ordnance Rifle); Sunshine Pics/ Alamy, p. 11 (1857 Model Napoleon); Popular Graphic Arts/ Wiki Commons, p. 12; Stocktrek Images/ Alamy, p. 13; Heritage Images/ Getty Images, pp. 14-15; Archive Photos/ Getty Images, p. 15; George Peter Alexander Healy/ Wiki Commons, p. 16; Bettmann/ Getty Images, p. 17; H. Armstrong Roberts/ ClassicStock/ Getty Images, pp. 18-19; Lithograph by Currier and Ives/ Wiki Commons, p. 18 (1861 entry); Nathaniel Currier and James Merritt Ives/ Wiki Commons, p. 19 (1863 entry); Granger record/ Wiki Commons, p. 19 (1865 entry); SueC, back cover.